THE BIG BOOK OF

TENNIS

FACTS

(for kids and adults)

D1301941

VALERIE POLLMANN R.

To my mum, who's passion for the sport,

made me love tennis.

Contents

Introduction

Tennis is one of the five most popular and played sports in the world. Men and women of all ages practice it in singles, doubles and mixed doubles. There is also a wheelchair category and it even has a professional tournament for seniors or over 35 year old players. It is perhaps today the most transversal sport that exists.

Like other sports, it is a game that exercises body and mind. There have been matches that have lasted days, and to arise victorious, players must not only be in great physical condition but also great mental state. It is one of the reasons why I admire and enjoy this sport so much. I've watched players overcome adversity and sometimes have huge comebacks surprising spectators and the contender with a victory that many had perhaps given for lost.

And, like many other sports, it gives players a chance for a rematch. Players who've lost consecutive finals against the same opponent have been able to eventually defeat their fears and adversaries to be crowned champions.

I have been lucky enough to watch two Grand Slam finals, and being there inspired me to gather all these interesting facts about this great sport.

Are you a tennis fan? Then this book is for you!

Everything about tennis since its beginnings

...

It is commonly believed that tennis was invented in England, but the "jeu de paume" (palm game) that was played in France in the 12th century is considered as a precursor.

•••

The word tennis comes from the French "tenez", which translates to "take" or "receive".

•••

Professional tennis is played on grass, clay and cement or hard courts.

•••

Before 1903 women's tennis was played only from the baselines. Hazel Hotchkiss Wightman introduced net and volley play in San Francisco and earned the nickname "Queen Mother of Tennis".

•••

Women's professional tennis began in 1926, but ended in 1927 and women did not compete as professionals until 1941. Exhibition matches took place again in 1947, but there was virtually no women's tennis until 1967 when Billie Jean King, Ann Jones, Françoise Dürr and Rosie Casals signed up to join an eight-man tour for two years.

•••

The song - Philadelphia Freedom - by Elton John is a tribute to Billie Jean King.

•••

Tennis is known as the "white sport", because in the beginning players only wore clothes of this colour.

•••

The shortest tennis match in tennis history lasted 18 minutes when Jack Harper defeated J. Sandiford 6-0, 6-0 at the 1946 Surrey Open Hard Court Championship.

•••

In 1958 the first tennis video game was invented. It was called "Tennis for two" and convincingly showed the movement of the ball when it passed over the net.

•••

The Open Era, where professional players could compete with amateurs, began in 1968.

•••

1972 was the year when the International Tennis Federation (ITF) was formed.

•••

In 1976 former acrobat skier, 18-year-old Brad Parks, suffered an injury that left him paraplegic. During his rehabilitation, he met wheelchair athlete Jeff Minnenbraker and the two began discussing the possibilities of wheelchair tennis.

•••

In 1981, the Wheelchair Tennis Players Association (WTPA) was formed.

•••

1988 was the year that the International Wheelchair Tennis Federation (IWTF) was founded at a meeting during the US Open.

•••

Tennis balls date back to the 15th century, they were made of leather and stuffed with wool or hair. Nowadays, tennis balls are usually of bright colours like green or neon yellow, so they are clearly visible. The balls have felt-like finish.

•••

Only Wimbledon maintained the tradition of white balls until 1986, the year in which they adopted the yellow colour ones in the tournament.

•••

As per the ITF, the weight of a tennis ball must be between 56.0 and 59.4 grams.

•••

Balls are replaced after every seven to nine games to make sure they are in perfect shape throughout the match. Those that are not in use are even stored in a refrigerated container to keep them in optimal conditions.

•••

Approximately 300 million balls are produced each year, which contributes around 22,000 tons of difficultly biodegradable rubber waste.

•••

There are more than 200 tennis ball brands that have been approved by the ITF.

•••

The ball is usually only in play for 20 minutes in an average, two-and-a-half-hour tennis match.

•••

Did you know that the tiebreak was invented by the chairman James Van Alen in 1965?

•••

Originally, Van Alen introduced two types of tiebreakers in the game. The one that would end after a maximum of 9 points was called "sudden death tiebreaker", while the one with 12 points was called "persistent death imbalance". The 12-point tie-break continues until a player or team wins by a margin of at least two points and with a minimum of 7 points.

•••

There is no definitive reason why we say "love" for zero in tennis. Some think it comes from the French expression "l'oeuf" as in "egg" meaning zero.

•••

The word racquet derives from Arabic word "rakhat" which means the palm of the hand.

•••

"Deuce" comes from "à deux le jeu" which means "to both is the game".

•••

Previously, tennis players racquets were smaller and made of wood. The racquet strings came from the sheep intestine tissue. Now they are made of steel and the strings are made of synthetic material.

•••

A wooden racquet was last used at Wimbledon in 1987.

•••

The overall permissible length of a tennis racquet is 29 inches (74 cms).

•••

The vast majority of the world's tennis racquets are manufactured in Asia, with Japan serving as the hub of international tennis racquet production.

•••

The best quality racquets are sold without strings, as experienced players prefer to decide what strings should be used and at what tension they should be strung.

•••

The ITF banned the "spaghetti string" racquet design in the 1980's, as this racquet improved players games to such an extent that low ranked players using it were consistently able to defeat more skilled players.

•••

In the beginning, tennis courts were hourglass shaped. Rectangular courts have been in existence since 1875.

•••

A standard tennis court is 27 feet wide for singles (8.23 mts) and 78 feet long (23.77 mts). The net is 3 feet 6 inches high (0.914 mts). For doubles, the width is 36 feet (10.97 mts) while the length remains the same.

•••

While on average most tennis rallies on all surfaces last lesser than 10 seconds, in 1984, Vicki Nelson-Dunbar and Jean Hepner played out a point which lasted 29 minutes. This came in one of the tie breaks, during which the ball crossed the net 643 times, before Nelson finally put it away for good with a short lob.

•••

Ever wondered where the 15, 30, 40 scoring system comes from? One theory is that clock faces were originally used to keep tabs on the score, with a quarter move of the hand to indicate 15, 30, and 45, and game over when the hand moved to 60. But, in order to ensure that a game couldn't be won by a one point difference, the concept of "deuce" was created. The movement to 45 on the clock face was changed to 40, and subsequent winning points would move the clock hands to 50, then 60. If a player failed to win two consecutive points, the clock would move back to 40, or "deuce".

•••

The world's highest tennis court is in the luxurious Burj al Arab hotel in Dubai, located 692 ft (211 mts) above sea level.

•••

Can you imagine tennis without a net? In the past, only a rope was used to separate the halves of the court.

•••

In March 2006 at the Nasdaq-100 Open, the hawk's eye was officially used for the first time in a tennis event.

•••

There are only 3 official hawk eyes, which move from tournament to tournament, according to the importance of these.

•••

Aussie player Sam Groth holds the record for the fastest serve in men's tennis. He sent the ball flying 163.4 mph (263 km/h) at the Busan Open Challenger Event in 2012. Second record belongs to Frenchman Albano Olivetti (257.5 km/h or 160 mph).

•••

A record of 303 weeks as world number 1 is held by tennis player Roger Federer, behind him appears the already retired U.S player Pete Sampras, with 286.

•••

The most successful doubles team in history are North American twins Bob and Mike Bryan. They have made a total of 166 finals together and hold a 112-54 record.

•••

John McEnroe and Stefan Edberg are the only players who have
managed to be number one in singles and doubles.

•••

Wheelchair tennis is one of the forms
of tennis adapted for wheelchair users. The size of the court, net
height, racquets, are the same, but there are two major differences
from pedestrian tennis: athletes use specially designed wheelchairs,
and the ball may bounce up to two times, where the second bounce
may also occur outside the court.

•••

Sport wheelchairs are lightweight, averaging 20 pounds (9 kilos), to a standard wheelchair's 35 pounds (15.8 kilos) and built for manoeuvrability.

•••

The quad division is restricted to players whose upper limbs are also impaired.

•••

In 2011, Andy Roddick made an appearance in Adam Sandler's comedy film Just Go With It with his real-life wife Brooklyn Decker.

•••

Swiss tennis player Martina Hingis became the youngest player in history to reach number 1 in the world at 16 years old in 1997.

•••

In 1977, women's tennis was the first professional sport open to transgender women. Renée Richards is the only person in history who participated in both the men's circuit and the women's circuit, after a sex reassignment surgery.

•••

Roger Federer is a man of many talents. In addition to being one of the greatest sportsmen of all times, and a good swimmer, Federer also has musical pursuits! He took up the piano as a youngster, and is said to continue playing it to this day, although he has not played in public before. He also plays the violin.

•••

While tennis singles is considered a battle of wits between two competing players, tennis doubles focuses more on the teamwork and partnership aspects of the game.

•••

In the men's game, Roger Federer has won 20 Grand Slam singles titles (until January 28, 2018) while on the women's side, Margaret Court has 24 singles majors.

•••

Rafael Nadal plays with his left hand even though he was born right-handed. His uncle taught him to hold a tennis racquet with his left hand when Nadal was 12 years old. He explained that the left-handed players can enjoy an advantage over their right-handed opponents because they're uncomfortable to play with as they strike into the opposite direction and can make the ball whirl in an inconvenient way for the right-handed players.

•••

Suzanne Lenglen was one of the greatest and first elite athletes in the world. She won six Wimbledon and twice the French Open. In 1997 she was paid tribute by placing her name on one of the Roland Garros courts and naming the women's trophy currently known as the Suzanne Lenglen Cup.

•••

In his 18-year pro career, Federer has not once retired mid-match.

•••

In 1970, women's tennis players were offered US$7,500 in prize money versus men's US$50,000 reward, which lead Billie Jean King and Casals to urge women to boycott.

•••

Monica Seles and Jimmy Connors are generally considered as the "grunt creators" in the women's and men's games respectively.

•••

The loudest grunt of 105db (decibels) came from the "Scream Queen" Maria Sharapova during 2009 Wimbledon. Just for reference, a normal conversation is registered at between 60 and 70db, and her grunt was louder than a train (90db), motorcycle (100db), lawnmower, police whistle, busy city traffic or noisy factory machinery.

•••

Anna Kournikova never won a single Professional Tournament in singles in her entire professional career. She did win 16 doubles titles though, including two Grand Slam titles after she partnered up with Martina Hingis at Australian Open in 1999 and 2002. This is why poker players named Ace-King combination after her - it looks good, but almost never wins.

•••

Del Potro has said if he wasn't a tennis player he would have pursued a career in architecture.

•••

The most noticeable and strange match took place in 2007. Roger Federer is considered "the king of grass", whereas Rafael Nadal is considered "the king of clay". A special court was constructed in such a way that one side was made out of grass and another side was made out of clay. Both players had to change sneakers each time when changing sides. Nadal won that time in three sets.

North American Billie Jean King was 39 years old when she won the singles tournament in Birmingham in 1983. She is still the most veteran player to win a tennis title.

Andre Agassi was the king of the hard court, collecting 40 outdoor hard court titles. For women, Chris Evert claimed 53!

In 1976, Chris Evert was named "Sportswoman of the Year" by the famous Sports Illustrated magazine, one of the only four occasions in which the award has been given to a tennis player.

•••

1981 was a very special year. It was the year when Roger Federer was born. Other tennis players who were born that same year include Anna Kournikova, Lleyton Hewitt, Anastasis Myskina, Serena Williams, Feliciano Lopez, Nikolay Davidenko, Alicia Molik, Mardy Fish, Jarkko Nieminen and others.

•••

In February 2013, Serena became the oldest woman, at 31 years, to be ranked world No.1. She re-set her own record when she returned to world No.1 on 30 January 2017 at 35 years, four months of age.

•••

Martina Navratilova wrote three mystery novels inspired by the world of tennis with famous writer Liz Nickles: The Total Zone (1994), Breaking Point (1996) and Killer Instinct (1997).

•••

The multilingual Federer speaks English, German, Swiss German and French. He's also a dual citizen; holds both Swiss and South African citizenship, the latter due to his mother, Lynette, having been born in South Africa.

•••

In 2014 Amelie Mauresmo succeeded Lendl as coach of Andy Murray, becoming the first woman to coach a top-10 male player.

•••

Tennis champion Roger Federer once considered becoming a professional soccer player.

•••

Nadal's a big fan of Real Madrid, he wants to be the president of the club in the future.

•••

Serena William has been a guest start on several popular tv shows such as *The Bernie Mac Show, ER, My Wife and Kids, Law & Order: Special Victims Unit, Street Time, The Division* and *Drop Dead Diva*. She has also shared her vocal talents in animated shows like *The Simpson, Higglytown Heroes* and *Avatar: The Last Airbender*.

•••

The Argentinean Guillermo Vilas, won 47 clay court tournaments during his career. Rafael Nadal, the current king of clay, could possibly break this record one day. For the women, it was Chris Evert again, claiming 66 clay titles, making her the most dominant tennis player on both hard and clay court!

•••

North American Jimmy Connors won 109 singles titles in his incredible career, which included 8 Majors.

•••

Mike Bryan has bested his twin brother Bob by 2 titles, having 107 in total, though that figure continues to grow each year!

•••

With 167 singles titles and 177 doubles titles, a collection of Grand Slams of 18 individual titles, 31 doubles and 10 mixed doubles accumulated in her 31-year career, Martina Navratilova predominates over her peers.

In 2017 Alexander Zverev (no.4) and Mischa Zverev (no. 33) became the first brothers in the year-end Top 35 in singles since 1991.

•••

Jack Sock (no. 8 singles, no. 39 doubles), Carreno Busta (no. 10 singles, no. 44 doubles), Pablo Cuevas (no. 32 singles, no. 21 doubles), Feliciano Lopez (no. 36 singles, no. 24 doubles) and Ryan Harrison (no. 47 singles, no.16 doubles) are the only five players who ended the year (2017) in Top 50 of both singles and doubles.

•••

Primarily known for his singles achievements, Federer has also won eight doubles titles – yet none since 2008. The biggest of those came at the Beijing 2008 Olympics (gold with Stanislas Wawrinka) and the 2003 Miami Masters (with Max Mirnyi).

•••

One of the most extroverted chair umpires is Mohamed Lahyani, a very popular one who often cheers the crowd.

•••

Chair umpires are classified with coloured badges. The first badge that a judge can win is the white one that allows him or her to officiate at the highest level within their own country.

•••

Do you know what badge colour is mandatory if an umpire wants to officiate a Grand Slam final? - The Golden Badge.

•••

For the first time at the 2015 US Open, the men's final was overseen by a woman, Eva Asderaki-Moore made history as chair umpire for the Federer - Djokovic championship title.

•••

In 1973, the US Open made history by being the first tournament to offer equal prize money to men and women. The prize money became equal for men and women in 2007 at Wimbledon.

•••

There are five line judges on each side of the court and each has only one line to monitor. The 10 line judges watch together two baselines, two central service lines, two horizontal service lines. Before the technology was developed to detect a ball that cut the network during a service, there was another judge sitting by the net. This judge grabbed the end of the net and tried to detect any vibration (or hear a noise) as the ball passed.

•••

Justine Henin retired in May 2008 while ranked world No. 1, just two weeks before the start of the French Open, at age 25.

•••

ITF Seniors Circuit consists of over 380 tournaments staged in more than 72 countries on all continents, with almost 25,000 players taking part each year.

Grand Slams and Summer Olympics

•••

The Grand Slam of tennis is formed by the four major tournaments of the international circuit organized by the International Tennis Federation, these are: Australian Open (hard court), French Open (red clay court), Wimbledon (grass court) and US Open (hard court).

•••

The player who manages to win the four major tournaments in the same year is said to have won the Grand Slam.

•••

Only two men completed a Grand Slam: Don Budge (1938), and Rod Laver, who did it twice (1962, 1969).

•••

As for women's singles players, only three did it: Maureen Connolly (1953), Margaret Court (1970) and Steffi Graf (1988).

•••

If a player wins all four tournaments at least once in his/her career, it is called as Career Grand Slam.

•••

Eight male players have completed the Career Grand Slam: Fred Perry, Don Budge, Rod Laver, Roy Emerson, Andre Agassi, Roger Federer, Rafael Nadal and Novak Djokovic.

Of those, only Agassi, Nadal, Federer and Djokovic have done it on 3 different surfaces. Of these 4, only Nadal has won at least 2 slams on each of the 3 surfaces.

•••

Ten female players completed the Career Grand Slam: Maureen Connolly, Doris Hart, Shirley Fry, Margaret Court, Billie Jean King, Chris Evert, Martina Navratilova, Steffi Graf, Serena Williams and Maria Sharapova.

•••

The first Wimbledon was played in 1877.

•••

The shortest tennis match in history of mere 20 minutes was played at Wimbledon in 1969 between Susan Tutt and Marion Bandy (Susan won 6-0, 6-0).

•••

The US Open was founded in 1881, the French in 1891, and the Australian in 1905.

•••

In 1917, the US Open was known as the Patriotic Tournament during the World War 1.

•••

Tennis was first played in the Summer Olympics in 1896, and then removed in 1924. In 1988 it was re-added to the Olympics as a real event.

•••

In 1992, wheelchair tennis became a full medal sport at the Paralympics in Barcelona, Spain for the first time with Pierre Fusade as Technical Delegate. Randy Snow of the USA and Monique van den Bosch of the Netherlands became double gold medallists, taking both singles and doubles titles.

•••

The first person to win Olympic gold in tennis was John Pius Boland of Ireland, who had no intention of competing in Athens, where he was vacationing. He got signed up for the singles tennis by a friend who was in the committee, so he entered and won. He then entered doubles tennis with the player he beat in Round 1 earlier and they won that gold, too.

•••

The first woman to win an Olympic event was England's Charlotte "Chattie" Cooper, who won the tennis singles at the 1900 games.

•••

In 1912, the Olympics and Wimbledon were held at the same time, and all of the best players chose to compete at Wimbledon.

•••

Serena and Venus Williams were the first sisters to win an Olympic medal in tennis.

•••

In London 2012, a mixed doubles event was officially included for the first time since 1924.

•••

Venus Williams is the only tennis player, male or female, to play in singles in five Olympic Games.

•••

John McEnroe won seven Grand Slam singles, nine Grand Slam doubles and one mixed double titles.

•••

The shortest Grand Slam final in history was when Steffi Graf beat Natasha Zvereva in just 34 minutes (6-0, 6-0) to defend her title at the 1988 French Open. The win came so easily and quickly, that Graf even apologized to the crowd in her speech, and years later she said that she felt regret for not letting Zvereva win at least a game or two.

•••

The longest Grand Slam final match lasted 5 hours and 53 minutes when Novak Djokovic defeated Rafael Nadal at the 2012 Australian Open. Both players nearly collapsed during the speeches.

•••

Tiffany & Co. makes the U.S. Open Trophy.

•••

The US Open is currently a hard court tournament, but it was formerly played on grass as well as on clay.

•••

Venus and Serena Williams are the only players with four gold medals in the history of the Summer Olympics. Venus was the singles champion in Sydney 2000. Serena won gold in London 2012. Together, in doubles, they climbed to the top of the podium three times. In Sydney 2000, in Beijing 2008 and in London 2012.

•••

Serena is also the only one who has won all four Grand Slam tournaments and Olympic gold medal during her singles and doubles career.

•••

Wimbledon is the only major tournament that is still played on grass.

•••

Roland Garros, the stadium where the French Open is played, is named after a French pilot of the First World War.

•••

Commonly, the official who has the honour of being the chair umpire of a Grand Slam tennis final is from the host country of the tournament.

•••

In 1971 – the tiebreak was introduced in Wimbledon.

•••

In the Australian Open, French Open, and Wimbledon, the final set of a match can go on and on until someone wins by two games over their opponent. The US Open is unique in that the final set of a match will be decided in a tiebreak game.

•••

Venus and Serena Williams became the first sisters to play each other in the 2001 US Open final.

•••

British Kitty McKane is the tennis player with the highest number of medals achieved: five. She was bronze in Antwerp in 1920 and in Paris in 1924 in singles. Gold in Antwerp and silver in Paris in doubles. And silver in mixed doubles in Antwerp.

•••

On the second day of the Wimbledon tournament in 2010, John Isner and Nicolas Mahut arrived to the court after 6pm ready to play their first-round singles match. Shortly after 9pm, the players had secured two sets each and the game was suspended until the next day. The following afternoon at 2pm, they started the fifth set. 3 hours and 40 minutes later, the match became the longest in tennis history, with scores tied at 32-32. When the score reached 47-47, the scoreboard stopped working! Shortly after 9pm, with a score of 59-59, the game was again suspended until the next day. The afternoon of the third day of the match, after an additional hour of play, Isner emerged victorious with a score of 70-68. With the final set that lasted more than 8 hours, the longest game of all time consisted of 183 games and an execution time of 11 hours and 5 minutes!

•••

In that same game the most aces during a match was registered: 113 by Isner, but Mahut also made enough (103 in total), between both players they made 223 aces.

•••

In the earlier years of Wimbledon, women wore full-length dresses.

Hazel Hotchkiss Wightman
circa 1910

•••

Henry "Bunny" Austin was the first player to wear shorts at
Wimbledon in 1932.

•••

The 2002 Australian Open became the first mainstream Grand Slam to have an NEC Wheelchair Tennis Tour event running directly alongside it.

•••

Serena Williams has won the most Grand Slams (23) in the Open Era, beating tennis legend Steffi Graf.

•••

In 2005 Wimbledon staged the first ever wheelchair tennis tournament on grass for eight of the world's leading men's doubles players. In September that same year, the US Open at Flushing Meadows became the third Grand Slam to stage a wheelchair tennis tournament alongside its main event.

•••

In 2007, after three successive years of wheelchair tennis exhibitions in Paris, Roland Garros became the last of the four Grand Slams to integrate competitive wheelchair tennis events.

•••

Althea Gibson was the first African-American to play in the U.S. Open Championship in 1950.

●●●

Arthur Ashe was the first African American to win the US open. He won the tournament for the first and only time in 1968. He said:

"Start where you are. Use what you have. Do what you can."

•••

Rufus – a Harris Hawk – is stationed at Wimbledon to keep its sky clear of local pigeons. Would you believe that this hawk has 5000 followers on Twitter?

•••

In 1973, US Open made history by being the first tournament to offer equal prize money to men and women. At Wimbledon 2007, the prize money became equal for men and women.

•••

The only two male singles players who have managed to win the four Grand Slam, the Davis Cup and the Olympic gold are the North American Andre Agassi and Spaniard Rafael Nadal.

•••

Boris Becker is the youngest male player ever to win a Wimbledon title. He was 17 years old in 1985 when he won it.

•••

In 1998 during the Australian Open, Venus and Serena Williams, who were 17 and 16 years old at the time, respectfully, declared that they would beat any man who was in the ATP 200 players. Venus was in the top 10 and Serena in the 20s. German player Karsten Braasch, ranked 203rd, accepted the challenge and defeated Venus in the first set 6-2 and Serena in the second 6-1. When the match was over he stated that he didn't do his best at all, and that he played as if he was ranked 600th. He even got a few puffs of cigarette and a few gulps of beer during the changeovers.

•••

Goran Ivanisevic is the only grand slam champion whose name alternates consonants and vowels.

•••

At Wimbledon, the grass is cut to a height of exactly 8 mm during the event.

•••

Jimmy Connors is the only player in history to have won US Open singles titles on all three surfaces (grass '74, clay '76 and hardcourt '78), and Chris Evert is the only woman to win it on two surfaces (clay, hardcourt).

•••

In a 2007 US Open match, Roger Federer went through 105 consecutive points without making an unforced error!

•••

Stefan Edberg was the first player ever to win a Career Junior Grand Slam. In 1983 he won the Australian Open, French Open, Wimbledon and US Open junior events in singles!

•••

With a capacity of 23,200 spectators, the "Arthur Ashe Stadium", a tennis stadium with an outdoor retractable-roof in New York City, US, is the largest of its kind in the world. It is named after the world-renowned professional tennis player Arthur Robert Ashe.

•••

The first Australian Open men's singles was held in 1905 and women's in 1922.

•••

Maureen "Little Mo" Connolly of the USA has the distinction of becoming the first woman to complete a 'Grand Slam'. She won the Australian Open, French Open, Wimbledon and US Open in the year 1953.

In September 1999 Serena Williams became the only North American woman to win the Grand Slam title after Althea Gibson. Serena won the singles title at the US Open and one day later she teamed up with her sister Venus to win the doubles title as well.

•••

Tennis analysts and players considered Wimbledon's grass courts to be the fastest-playing surface of the Grand Slams and the clay courts at Roland Garros to be the slowest.

•••

Roger Federer won the 2017 Wimbledon without dropping a set, first time after '76 (Borg won the title then).

•••

In 2013, Andy Murray became the first British Wimbledon champion in 77 years.

•••

Japanese Kei Nishikori became the first Asian player to reach a men's Grand Slam final at the 2014 US Open.

•••

The Australian Open is usually held during the summer where temperatures rise up almost to 113°F (45°C). The 2007 edition was one of the hottest seasons of the Aus Open.

•••

In this tournament, if the temperature exceeds 95°F (35°C), by law the game must be stopped to protect players, umpires and ball boys/girls.

•••

The main court of the Roland Garros stadium was named in honour of Phillippe Chatrier. A man passionate about tennis who, despite not reaching a professional level, became a journalist to be close to the sport he loved so much. He was part of the federation and founded a magazine.

•••

Players must submit their clothing to the All England Lawn Tennis and Croquet Club for approval before participating in the Wimbledon championships.

•••

A player who wins an Olympic gold medal and all four Grand Slam events in the same year is said to have won a Golden Slam.

•••

Steffi Graf is the only tennis player in history, both male and female to complete a Golden Slam (she won all four Grand Slams and an Olympic gold medal in Seoul 1988).

•••

The US Open requires two different types of tennis balls, the extra-duty for the men and the regular duty for the women. The size, pressure, and design may be the same, but the difference of felt creates a large difference in speed and action.

•••

Ball boys and girls have the toughest jobs in the tournament because they need to have quick reflexes and keep track of the tennis balls. Months before a tournament begins the children start undergoing intensive training so that they are ready to take up this arduous task!

•••

The average age of Ball Boys/Girls who serve at Wimbledon is 15. Every year, 250 of these young kids are selected to serve at the tournament.

•••

One of the greatest comebacks was Goran Ivanisevic finally winning Wimbledon in 2001. Ivanisevic had already lost three Wimbledon finals to the two great North American players of his era: Andre Agassi (in 1992) and Pete Sampras (in 1994 and 1998), and after that third defeat, in five sets, he seemed to lose his way and his motivation. He plunged down the world rankings, and had to be granted a Wild Card to enter the tournament. He beat a series of fine players, including Marat Safin (who at that time was the reign champion), to reach the semi-final. He played the final against Australia's Pat Rafter and won 9-7 in the fifth set.

•••

The fact that he went on to win Wimbledon as a Wild Card, made him the only man ever to do so.

•••

Every year, 24 tons of strawberries are consumed during Wimbledon.

•••

Australian Ken Rosewall holds the record of being the oldest as well as the youngest man to win the Australian Open title. He became the youngest winner of the competition in 1953 at 18 years and two months when he defeated compatriot Mervyn Rose in straight sets to win the first Grand Slam title of his career. Coincidentally, Rosewall became the oldest champion of the tournament at 37 years and two months when he won the last Grand Slam title of his career. Once again he defeated a compatriot in the final in straight sets, this time Mal Anderson.

•••

Nadal is the youngest tennis player to complete both Career Grand Slam and Career Golden Slam.

•••

A Slazenger tennis ball, Wimbledon's official ball since 1902 must:
- Bounce between 53 and 58 inches (1.35 and 1.47 mts) after being dropped into concrete from a height of 100 inches (2.54 mts)
- Measure two-and-a-half inches (6.35cm) in diameter
- Weight two ounces (56.7g)
- Be treated with a water repellent barrier called Hydroguard (to protect it from the British rain)

- Be packed in a pressurized tin to keep it from going soft
- Be kept at 68°F (20°C) in a fridge, court side to keep them in perfect condition.

•••

The 2008 French Open saw the last appearance of former world number one, Brazilian Gustavo "Guga" Kuerten.

•••

The winner's trophy at Wimbledon remains on display at the All England Club's museum as winners do not take their trophies with them. However, they are given small replicas of the official trophies.

•••

The golden cup given to the men's winner at Wimbledon dates back to 1887, while the trophy given to women, called the "salver," dates back to 1864.

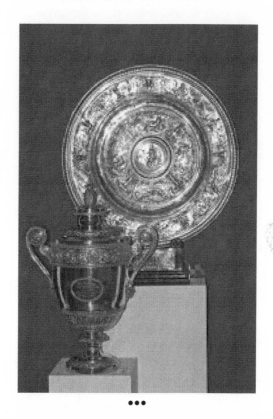

•••

A Pineapple, adorns the top of the Wimbledon's Men Singles Trophy. It represents English sailors who used to put pineapples outside their homes after returning from a long voyage.

•••

A funny incident happened during the US Open in 2014. The hair of Denmark's tennis star, Caroline Wozniacki got tangled with her racquet in the middle of the match but after this unwanted situation, the match did not stopped and she continued to play with tangled hair.

Since its inception in 1905, the Australian Open has been played in two different countries and a total of seven cities, five in Australia and seven in New Zealand. Melbourne became the official venue for the tournament in 1972 and the tournament has been staged there a total of 55 times. The other cities that have staged the Australian Open include Sydney, which hosted the tournament 14 times, Adelaide, which hosted it 17 times, Brisbane, seven times, and Perth, three times. Christchurch and Hastings are the two New Zealand cities that hosted the tournament in 1906 and 1912 respectively.

•••

Wimbledon is now one of the most-watched sporting events in the world, but back in its earliest days saw abysmally low numbers in attendance. There were only 200 spectators in the first Wimbledon tournament and the tickets were sold for one shilling (12 pence today) each in the final match.

•••

By defeating Angelique Kerber in the Olympic Games of Rio 2016. Monica Puig became the first Puerto Rican athlete to get an Olympic gold medal.

•••

The US Open became the first Grand Slam to have women in the umpire chair for both the men's and women's singles finals in its 2015 version.

•••

South African Kevin Anderson won the second-longest match in Wimbledon history by outlasting North American John Isner to reach the men's final. They played on Centre Court for six hours and 35 minutes before winning 7-6 (8-6) 6-7 (5-7) 6-7 (9-11) 6-4 26-24. The final set alone lasted for two hours and 50 minutes. With this he became the first south African man to reach Wimbledon singles final since 1921.

•••

The only two Olympic gold medals that Chile has obtained and the Olympic bronze medal of tennis players Nicolás Massú and Fernando González were known as "the feat of the Heroes of Athens" due to the few hours of rest between their clashes, because both advanced simultaneously to the finals in singles and doubles. On the second to last day in their matches for medals, the Chileans played about 15 hours out of 24.

•••

An estimated 54,250 tennis balls are used during the Wimbledon.

•••

Serena Williams is the first mother and professional tennis player to reach the last round of the Wimbledon tournament since Australian Evonne Goolagong in 1980.

•••

Only one professional tennis player who later became a mother during her career has won Wimbledon in over 100 years: the Australian Evonne Goolagong, aged 28, in 1980. In 1973, Margaret Court won the French, Australian and US Opens after giving birth to her son. While Kim Clijsters became the third mother to obtain a Grand Slam title in 2009, winning the US Open in front of a crowd that included her 18-month-old daughter.

•••

McEnroe became the youngest male winner at 20 years at the 1979 U.S Open.

•••

Björn Borg liked his racket strung at 80lbs pressure, which was too tight to achieve without breaking a string or twisting the frame. He trusted one stringer in the world, a fellow Swede called Mats Laftman. At such pressure they were vulnerable and Borg broke 60 strings during a French open.

ATP, WTA, Davis & Fed Cup

•••

The Association of Tennis Professionals (ATP) was formed in September 1972 by Donald Dell, Bob Briner, Jack Kramer, and Cliff Drysdale to protect the interests of male professional tennis players.

•••

A year later, Billie Jean King founded the Women's Tennis Association (WTA), to create a better future for women's tennis. Today, the WTA has more than 2,500 players from almost 100 countries competing.

•••

The Frenchman Julien Benneteau holds the inglorious record of winning 245 singles matches (lost 258 matches) without ever winning a single ATP tournament title.

•••

Jeļena Ostapenko became the first Latvian player of either sex to win a Grand Slam singles tournament, it was also her first WTA Tour-level singles title.

•••

Greek player Stefanos Tsitsipas made ATP history as the youngest man (19 years old) to defeat four top-10 players at a single tournament at the 2018 Rogers Cup.

•••

German Sabine Lisicki currently holds the record for the fastest service on the WTA, with a speed of 131 mph (210.8kph) at the 2014 Stanford Classic. Previously Venus Williams had this record with a speed of 120 mph (207.6kph) that she achieved at the 2007 US Open.

•••

Japanese Kimiko Date-Krumm is the oldest player, with 47 years, who is still active on the WTA circuits.

•••

In 2018 Roger Federer became the oldest male tennis player to reach world no. 1 since the introduction of the ATP Rankings in 1973.

•••

In 2008, Juan Martin Del Potro became the first player in ATP history to win his first four career titles in as many tournaments (Stuttgart, Kitzbuhel, Los Angeles and Washington, D.C.).

•••

Safin - Safina, the siblings and World N°1. It is not usual to find siblings who go far in the world of tennis. Having both become number 1 in the world, is almost impossible. But in Russia it happened, and Marat Safin and Dinara Safina were the ones who led the ATP and WTA rankings respectively.

•••

Standing 6 feet 11 inches tall (2.11 mts), Croatian Ivo Karlovic is the tallest player on the ATP tour.

•••

Standing 6ft' 3in" tall (1.90 mts), Czech Eva Hrdinová and the Uzbek Akgul Amanmuradova both share the record of being the tallest athletes among female tennis players.

•••

Diego Schwartzman, a 25-year-old Argentine who is five feet and seven inches (1.70m) tall. Has been nicknamed "El Peque" ("the small one").

•••

Francisco Clavet set an ATP tournament record in the first round of the 2001 Heineken Open Shanghai, when he defeated Jiang Shan in 25 minutes, 6-0, 6-0.

•••

Chilean Marcelo Rios was the first Latin American to become World No. 1 in the Open Era when he defeated Pete Sampras in March 1998.

•••

The WTA Finals is the tournament played annually at the end of the season for the top-ranked players on the Women's Tennis Association (WTA) tour.

•••

Since 2003 there have been eight singles players divided into two round robin groups, and eight doubles teams. Qualified players participate in a round-robin format in two groups of four. The winners and runners-up of each group advance to the semi-finals. Doubles teams participate in a single elimination draw.

•••

Spaniard Arantxa Sanchez-Vicario qualified for the WTA Finals 13 times throughout her distinguished career.

•••

Chris Evert was the winner of the first edition of the WTA finals in 1972, prevailing in the clay of Boca Raton against Kerry Melville Reid in the final, with only 17 years.

•••

Martina Navratilova is the player with more appearances in the history of the WTA finals, participating in 21 editions between 1974 and 1994. She is also the most successful player in the WTA finals with eight individual titles, including five consecutive titles from 1983 until 1986.

•••

Monica Seles won the WTA Finals three times in a row from 1990 to 1992. She lost the 2000 final to Martina Hingis.

In 2009, ATP introduced a new tour structure called ATP World Tour consisting of ATP World Tour Masters 1000, ATP World Tour 500, and ATP World Tour 250 tier tournaments, the Tennis Masters Series tournaments became the new Masters 1000.

•••

The Masters 1000 tournaments are Indian Wells, Miami, Monte Carlo, Madrid, Rome, Toronto/Montreal, Cincinnati, Shanghai and Paris.

•••

By defeating Roger Federer in the final in Cincinnati 2018, Novak Djokovic became the only player in history to complete a "Career Golden Master", winning the 9 Masters 1000 tournaments in his career.

•••

The ATP World Tour Finals is the culmination of the tennis season as the final men's event of the year. The top eight men earn the right to compete at the event. A player can also qualify if they won a Grand Slam but finished in the top 20.

•••

Doubles is also an equal part of the ATP World Tour Finals. After having its own separate event for many years, the year-end doubles championships was combined with the singles event for the first time in 2003 at Houston with Bob and Mike Bryan winning in five sets over Michael Llodra and Fabrice Santoro.

•••

Andre Agassi leads all players in terms of most years qualified to the ATP World Tour Finals at a record 14 times with his last appearance being in 2003.

•••

Only three players have won the event without losing a match: Michael Stich in 1993, Lleyton Hewitt in 2001 and Roger Federer in 2003, 2004, 2006, 2010, and 2011.

•••

Boris Becker and Pete Sampras clashed in the 1996 ATP World Tour finals that ended with Sampras winning 3-6, 7-6(5), 7-6(4), 6-7(11), 6-4 in a match considered one of the greatest of that decade.

•••

The Davis Cup is the only team tournament in the world which has lasted a full century.

•••

The competition began in 1900 as a challenge between Great Britain and the United States. The tournament was designed in 1899 by four members of the Harvard University tennis team, Dwight Davis amongst them, who wanted to challenge the British to a tennis competition. Davis died in 1945. Following his death, the cup was named the Davis Cup.

•••

The women's equivalent of the Davis Cup is the Fed Cup. Australia, the Czech Republic, and the United States are the only countries to have held both Davis Cup and Fed Cup titles in the same year.

•••

The history of Fed Cup takes us back to the year 1919 when Hazel Hotchkiss Wightman came up with an idea to have a team championship for women. But the idea was promptly rejected. So just like in the lines of Davis Cup she presented a trophy on her own in 1923 and started an annual contest between the United States and Great Britain female players.

•••

The Hopman Cup, is a third competition for mixed teams, carries less prestige, but is a popular curtain raiser to the tennis season.

•••

In 1982, John McEnroe of the US and Mats Wilander of Sweden played the longest singles match in Davis Cup history. The match lasted 6 hours and 22 minutes.

•••

The United States has won 7 consecutive Davis Cup titles (1920 - 1926).

•••

The Davis cup first adopted the tiebreak in all sets except the final set in 1989, and made amendments in their rules to adopt the tiebreakers for all five sets in 2016.

•••

From 1905 to 1914 Australia and New Zealand sent a combined team to play in the Davis Cup as "Australasia".

•••

The United States has won the most number of championships in both the Davis and Fed Cup.

•••

In 1974 both South Africa and India reached the Davis Cup finals for the first time ever. They even became the first non-American and Non Europe teams. But because South African government's apartheid politics, India refused to compete and South Africa was declared winner by default. But since then South Africa has never reached the finals of the Davis Cup.

•••

In 2017, 125 nations competed in the Davis Cup, which makes this the world's largest sports competition.

•••

Tennis is usually an individualistic sport, but the Fed and Davis Cup offer players the possibility to play for their country in a joint team.

Other books by Valerie Pollmann R.

150 Most Beautiful French Quotes
Translated into English

Amazing Facts about FIFA World Cup

I hope you have enjoyed reading and learning more about this ancient sport.

If you liked the book or have any comments, leave your review on Amazon. I personally read all reviews, to continue writing what people want to read.

Thanks for your support!

35532352R00059

Made in the USA
Middletown, DE
07 February 2019